THE
VOICES
OF THE
HEART

POEMS OF INSPIRATION

Pauline Esbery

THE
VOICES
OF THE
HEART

POEMS OF INSPIRATION

Pauline Esbery

Kravitz & Sons

INNOVATORS IN PUBLISHING, MARKETING AND ADVERTISING

Kravitz and Sons LLC
1301 Farmville Blvd, Suite 104
Greenville, NC 27834

Published by Kravitz and Sons LLC.

ISBN: 979-8-89639-108-1 (sc)
ISBN: 979-8-89639-107-4 (e)

Library of Congress Control Number: 2025903458

Table of Contents

Humility is the strength of a good character.

Acknowledgment

I thank God for the inspirations He gave me to create a purpose and will in my life.

The many life experiences He allows me to attain and retain in order to write this book.

I thank my children for their encouragement that fuels the fire in my soul.

To my grandchildren "my future" I dedicated this book to them. I pray that they will fight their battles with pens and paper.

My editors, I thank you both for giving life to these words.

To all my friends who are a constant source of strength and support I appreciate you all.

WITH ALL HIS BLESSINGS, THANKS A MILLION!

AND WE CRY 'ABBA'

* * * * *

PRAYERS NEVER FAILS
WHEN IT IS DONE RIGHT,
WHEN IT IS ASKED ACCORDING TO GOD'S WILL.

TRUE LOVE

Yesterday, our spirits met and held hands.

Today our hearts melt into one from the flickering flames of our love. God held the one heart in the palm of His hand and Declared, "Let no man separate what I have joined together."

Now this heart Speaks as one, Laughs as one, Cries as one. Walks as one. This love is now sealed with fire of love. Savored with salt of tears that brings joy.

Crowned with humbleness and respect one for the other. Trust takes on new meaning when two hearts become one.

Tomorrow, love will continue to flow from our hearts, not for us to see, but for you to feel the warmth of our love.

This love stared in heaven above, sealed with the approval of God.

Angels sings when God's will is done on earth.

Don't you know that true love comes from God?

ALONE

I am standing in the desert, the heat is closing in.
There is no wind of hope,
My soul is troubled, there is no peace.
I am standing all alone, with no one to look to.

I tried looking up.
But my burden weights me down.
I try looking within, but it is hard to see.
I felt no compassion, it's dark and cold.

I open my mouth to pray, but the only word I could say is,

"Jesus"
So, I cried
"JESUS! JESUS!"

As I cried Jesus, my burden started to get lighter.
Peace, hope, and joy started to flood my soul.
Tears came freely.

I gave way to a language, that God alone could understand.
Then a settled peace came over me,
as God reminded me of His promise in Isaish 41:10.

"Fear thou not, for I am With thee,
be not dismayed, For I am Thy God, I will Strengthen thee,
yea I will Help thee, I will uphold Thee with the right hand
of my righteousness."

THE CRY

I hear the cry, why me?
But don't cry, trust me.
I know you.

I made you in my own image.
So, I know your fears, pain and loneliness.
I know the cruelty of man.
Trust Me, I walked this earth before.

Love Me, give yourself to me.
I will love you.
I will take your pain.

And if you believe in Me, I will heal you.
I can give you life.
I can give you love.
I can give you hope.
I can give you peace.

That passes all understanding.

Call on Me, My name is JESUS.

FATHER'S DAY

This is Father's Day, but where is my Fattier?
Where is the man that fashioned me in my mother's womb?

I thank God that He allows us to call Him Father. I thank God
that He promises that He will never leave us nor forsake us.
I know with all my heart and soul, That my Heavenly Father
cares for me.

I need your hug father, I need your smile, I need to look in your
eyes, to see if yours are the same color as mine.

I search faces on the street, looking for one that resembles mine.
I smile at fathers. Hoping my smile will remind you of the
woman you slept with when I was conceived...My Mother.

Father, where are you?
Do you ever think about me?
Do you remember the night I was conceived?
Do you know or care about the hurt, the pain;
The heart that is burdened with pain of not knowing you?
Did your father do the same to you?

TAKE HEART

It will not end as it began, come, accept Jesus' promises.
He will show you how it will be.

First, give up all.
Accept Jesus Christ as the Lord of your life.
Then, you will know your life will not end as it began.

TO THE HOMELESS…you will have a mansion that,
Jesus has gone to prepare for you.

TO THE HUNGRY…all you can eat buffet fit for a king.
TO THE SICK…there is healing in His wings.
TO THE NAKED…a royal robe awaits you.
TO THE SORROWFUL…there are no more tears or sorrow.
TO THE POOR…there are riches untold in heaven,
And you will receive your own.

Remember, you are now joint heir to the throne with Jesus.

I AM YOURS

I am your daughter.
You have chosen me.
You gave me the right to call you Father.

You made me "Heir, Joint Heir" to the throne.
You gave me the right to call Jesus, my brother.

GOD IS ABLE

Put down your trouble,
Give them to God.
He will do His will. He knows what to do.
Troubles are like fire that burns the heart.
It brings tears to the eyes.

God is able. God is good.
He takes care of all.
He will give you joy and peace of mind.
He will take all your troubles and turn them into JOY.

GRACE

My tears will turn to joy
My heart will lift with gladness
When I see the glory of God.
The pain I bore, I do not remember.
The confusion of the mind is way behind.
Fears are no more.
You see, I claimed boldly from the Throne of Grace.

Grace that will get me to the everlasting life.
Serving my God, my King.
All praise and glory to my Lord.
With open arms I received my all,
From my Father who promises me all.
Gods' grace is sufficient.

Read 2 Corrrinthians12:9

HE CARES

In thy arms, I place my cares.
At thy feet, I lay my claims.
I know, You will answer.
My Lord, who cares.

I know You care.
With my heart, I give Thee thanks.
With my voice, I shout "Thy praise.
I praise Thee, Lord with
My soul.
My heart.
My mind."

Read 1 Peter 5:7

THANK YOU LORD

Thank You Lord

I thank You Lord for today.
I thank You for a true life in Thee.
A life Lord, I know will go on forever.
How do I know Lord?

You told me so.
You said that anyone who believes in Your Son,
Jesus Christ shall not perish but have eternal life.

I know Lord,
You cannot lie, and You will not go back on your words.
You cannot do that. You are the Great and Holy I AM.

I TAKE WITH YOU

Lord, with each step I take I want to step with You.
Lord, each word I say I want it to be Yours.
Lord, with each action I want it to be Your direction.

I enter each day Lord with gladness of heart, mind and soul.
Knowing Lord that You will never leave me nor forsake.

Each happiness, I take with You.
Each problem, I take with You.
Each sorrow, I take with You.
Thank You Lord always being there.
At all the right times.

IN MY TIME

The child cried.
"Heal me Lord"
The Lord said.
"not yet my child"
The child cried,
"Let me walk"
The Lord said.
"I know that you need that touch"

The child cried.
"When will that be?"
The Lord said
"In my time, in my time"
In my time, I will deliver.
In my time I will do,
I want it to be known that My time is not your time.
In My time I will do My will.
I will give you grace in your time to wait upon
Me to work in my time.

HE IS WITH ME

I passed through the river
But it did not flow over me.
I passed through the fire
I came out pure as gold.
I walked through the land of darkness.
But no evil came near me.
Because at the name of Jesus every demon flees.

My Lord Jesus was with me all the way.
I planted my footsteps in His.
I spoke when He told me to.
I turned when He wanted me to.
I sat when He wanted me to.
I prayed how He wanted me to pray.

Thank God,
I have become a follower behind the greatest leader.
If I did not.
The river would overflow me.
The fire would have burned me.
Evil would have overcome me.
I would be without hope, joy, peace or life everlasting.

JESUS

I fell along the way, You lifted me.
I was weary, You gave me strength.
I stumbled along the way,
You held my hands and showed me the narrow way.
In my trouble heart, You gave me peace.
When I cried, You read my tears.
Because You alone know the language of tears.
You showed compassion when I was hurt.
You showed mercy and forgiveness when I fell into temptation.

"Lord, I love you."
You have kept your promise to me.
Please help me to keep mine.
You are my Lord.
You are my King.
You are my Savior.
You are my Everything.

FAITH AND FEAR
CANNOT WALK HAND IN HAND.
ONE HAS TO GO FORWARD.
THE OTHER REMAIN ON THE OUTSIDE.

WHICH ONE WILL YOU CHOOSE TODAY?
FAITH OR FEAR.

DON'T

The peace You gave me Lord,
Don't let it pass away.
The love You gave me Lord.
Don't let it pass away.
The understanding You gave me Lord.
Don't let it pass away.
The ability of knowing Your will, Lord.
Don't let it pass away Lord.
I don't want to be removed from Your presence.
Where there are joys forever more.
Lord, I need to be with You always.

GENTLE TOUCH

Your gentle spirit touches my soul today.
It calms my aching heart.
It tells me You are near.
It tells me You have heard my cries.
"Your will, not my own."

Your gentle spirit gave me a new song.
A song of peace and love.
That heals every sickness.
A song that brings rest to my spirit.

A BABE

You came as a babe to us in such a humble way.
With angels proclaiming
This is your day.
This is the Christ we seek laying in a manger meek.
With gold, Frankincense, and myrrh at His feet.
A thousand voices raise, praising
The Newborn King.
He is the King of Kings.
He is the Lord of Lords.
He is the Son of God.
With grateful heart, we will sing His praises to this world of sin.

FILL ME UP

Lord, please start the healing, in my soul today.
Fill me with Your Holy Spirit.
 Lord starts the healing in my heart today.
I asked you today.
Please mend my heart.
Please heal my soul.
Fill it with thy love
Fill me with Your Holy Spirit I pray.

GIVE

Give, give unto Him.
Give your life to Him.
He is coming soon.
See the signs that cannot lie.
Famine, earthquakes, and war are everywhere.
What more do you want to know?
All you need to know …
Is to give your life to God.
He can save you and give you life everlasting.

YOU

BY YOU
By Your grace I am living.
By Your will I am doing.
By Your mercy I am existing.
By Your compassion I am feeling.
Resting daily on You is victory.

WITH YOU
With Your love I am loving.
With Your kindness I am giving.
With Your forgiveness I am forgiving.
With Your peace I am understanding.
Relying on Jesus is my daily task.

FOR YOU
For You, I am praising
For You, self is dying.
For You, songs are singing.
The just, must live by faith.

THROUGH YOU
Through You, the sickness is healed.
Through You, souls are saved.
Through You, victories are won.
Though You, Harvest is reaped.
We are nothing without Gods' help.

**THE HIGHWAY TO HEAVEN
HAS NO SPEED LIMIT.**

CRY NOT FOR ME

Cry not for me loved ones.
Take joy in the happy memories I left behind.
Forgive me for any hurt I may have caused.
But cry not for me.

Rejoice, I am gone to the Holy Nation.
Where there are no tears, sorrow or pain.
But there I will receive my key to my Mansion.
My new Name, my Ring, and my Royal Robe.
There, I will sup with the King of Kings.
And sing praises forever more.
Cry not for me.

When I hear the words
"Come my good faithful servant"
It will be worth every sorrow, loneliness and pain.
Keep my memory by loving, sharing, and giving one to the other.
But most of all.
Keep my memory by giving your life to Jesus.
Goodbye my loved ones.
Cry not for me.

WHEN A MAN ACTS LIKE A CHILD
IT FORCES THE WIFE TO ACT LIKE
LIKE HIS MOTHER.

THEN SHE LOSES HIM
BECAUSE HE DOES NOT WANT A MOTHER.
HE WANTS A WIFE

NO ORDINARY CITIZEN

I am no ordinary citizen.
I came for a purpose.
I came to tell of Gods' love.
I am no ordinary citizen.
I am just passing through.
To tell of His love, To tell of His grace.
So, please listen,
Jesus loves you so much.

He wants you to know, He died for your sins.
He wants you to know, He forgave every sin.
He wants you to know how much He loves you.

I am just passing through.
I am a citizen of a Holy Nation.
I am on my way home.
To walk on the streets of gold.
To receive my key to my mansion.
A place where there are no tears or sorrow.
Only joy and peace.
I am of, a peculiar people saved by grace.
Washed in blood that was shed for us.
I walk in faith and not by sight.
I am no ordinary citizen; I was bought with a price.

HAPPINESS

Happiness, pure joy and Happiness
Is found in Thee.
When I surrender my all to thee.
Happiness, pure joy and Happiness
Is found in Thee.
When I lift, my heart to Thee.
Happiness, pure joy and Happiness.
Is found in Thee.
When I lift praises to thee.
So, rejoice, lift your voices to the King of kings.
Come and praise, praise His Name today.
Because, He is the King, because He is the Lord.
Happiness, pure joy and Happiness.
Is found in Thee, when I look up to Thee.

I SHALL RISE

I shall rise
I shall rise
Don't leave me Lord.
I need Your Power and your Strength
To raise again.
I shall raise
I shall raise.
Dear Lord, Dear Lord, You promise,
You will never leave me nor forsake me.
Please Lord, Please Lord.
Stay by my side.
I need You now.
More than ever to be with me.
My Rock.

HER SON

I saw the grief.
I saw the tears.
I saw the pain.
That only a mother knows when, she has lost son to the gun.
Her son, the one that came from her womb.
Her son, the one she loves with all her heart, is taken away.

Her heart cries…
"tell my son I will be there, heavens' joy with him to share."
Tell my son I will be there.

GOD DOES HIS WORK
BY MOVING US TO DO OUR WORK.
FAITH IS THE HAND THAT TAKES THE THINGS WE NEED
FROM GOD.

A PIECE OF CLAY

He took a piece of clay.
He broke the clay.
Some parts were hard,
Some soft.
But He broke it in a tender loving way.
He held it in His hand and spoke.
He planned my destiny.
Only I did not have ears to hear them.
Nor heart to store His words.
He did not want me to hear them.
I would not have understood.
I would be afraid to.
I would not be able to live by faith,
If I knew all that he had instore for me.

Maybe I would plead with Him not to let me go.
Not to send me in this world of sin.
But to stay sheltered in His loving care.
With loving care and order.
He voiced the plan for my life.
He knew of the attack of the enemies.
He knew of my failure and my victories.
He knew that walking this road of life,
I would need Him all the way.
So, He made me a promise that,
He would never leave me nor forsake me.
Somehow, my ears heard these words and my heart stored them.

**FAITH WILL NOT WORK IN AN UNFORGIVING HEART.
GOD WILL BLESS YOUR NEEDS NOT YOUR GREED.**

THE EMPTY CHAIR

There was not enough on the plate.
I look at the empty chair at the head of the table.
Where is the chief provider?
Where are you, Dad?
I need you to be my hero.
You see Dad, I need you to show me how
To be a man.
I need you to teach me Dad,
How to be responsible from a man's point of view.

I went fishing, but your chair was empty.
There was no father to teach me how to reel in the fish.
I went to the game, but your chair was empty.
There was no father to shout with me at the game.
Your chair was empty.
It's empty at dinner time.
It's empty at prayer time.
I need you to teach me how to be the spiritual head of the house, I will have one day.
Dad where are you?
Your chair of Love, Protection, Provider and Friendship is empty.
Please Dad, come and take your rightful place at the table of my heart.
Your chair needs to be filled.

MESSENGER OF LOVE

She knew her mission, she answered the call.
She listened, she got her divine order, she obeyed,
Giving up all.
Love, compassion, and humbleness she kept.
Over the sick she wept.
As she cared for the sick with sores,
She did not keep scores.
Moving from one to the other she left her love of God,
To keep and sustain them.
She brought out the true meaning of being a brother's keeper.
She taught each one to care for each one.

Her humbleness and love of humanity,
opened doors to kings and queens and heads of states.
But greatest of all, the gates of Heaven are open wide for her.
Welcoming the Daughter of the 'MOST HIGH GOD.'

TODAY I WALK

Today I walked away from my best friend.
He is my soul mate.
He is the love of my life.
He is the flesh of my flesh.
But I had to walk.
I walked away with the laughter we shared together.
I walked away with the hope we had together.
I walked away with the tears we shed.
I walked away with the love that will always bind us together.

Gone is the hope of his life with mine.
Gone is my best friend.
Gone is the touch and feel of his skin next to mine.
Gone are the lips that smiled back at me.
Gone are the eyes that pierced my heart.
But I had to walk away.
My heart cries for the love of my life.
But I had to walk.
My Savior calls.

MY BIBLE

I felt numb as I looked intently at the spot in disbelief where my car was.
Was, it is not there.
Was, it was stolen.
By someone who does not want a car payment, insurance payment.
By someone who thinks he can find better use for my car.
By someone who did not spare a thought about my welfare.

Yes, my car was taken without question.
I thought about my stuff in the car.
My Bible, My weapon, My encourager,
My past, present, and future history.
I thought about the brown pages.
The used pages, the little notes here and there.
The highlights.

I cried.
Not for my car, but for my personal guide.
God, I said,
Let anyone who has my bible be convicted by the word.
Let the word come alive and pierce the heart as a two-edged sword.
Bring forth compassion.
Bring love and kindness to each other.
Bring salvation to everyone within your reach.
Lord, turn evil into good that your name be Glorified.

THE WILL OF GOD WILL NOT TAKE YOU WHERE THE GRACE OF GOD CANNOT KEEP YOU.

TRUST HIM.

MEND MY HEART

I cried from my heart.
My mouth did not speak a word.
My eyes shed tears that only God could see.
He heard, the sound of a broken heart.

My heart cried out,
Please Lord,
Mend this broken heart.
Take this pain and turn it into joy.
Fill this heart with love, forgiveness and peace.
And I will cry no more.

SOUL MATE

To every man, there is a woman.
To every woman, there is a man.
To find one's soul mate is a mystery.
The soul mate of each one, sometimes cannot be found.
There is war, accident, sickness, jail,
Acts of nature, mating with the wrong mate, to take each one.
Alas, each one has a different pathway and different motives
when one goes seeking.

Some go seeking without prayer and supplication,
Find the wrong mate and end up weeping.
Some out of desperation grab the first wrong mate.
Oh, if only they had waited on God to provide.
He would have allowed their soul mate to take their rightful
place by their side.
To each his own.
But each must wait, pray and prepare to receive.
Some compromise, I am too fat, I am getting old.
So, with one smile, one grasp, this is my last chance.
But, alas, beauty is in the eyes of the beholder, one should have
waited.

Oh, the money!
All that glitters is not gold.
One took without looking, it is not the soul mate one is seeking.
So the giving stopped coming right after the getting.

Ones' soul mate never stops giving.

When you find your soul mate you will know.

He will be everything to you, just as Jesus is everything to the church.

Jesus commanded the man to love his wife as He, Christ, loves the church.

As you know, Christ gave His life for the church.

Is there any greater love than when you find your soulmate

Through prayer and supplication?

NOT MY PLACE

You try to teach me the game.
I try to understand.
I clapped when others clapped.
I shouted when others shouted.
I did try to understand the game.
I tried not to look bored at the game for
I know your father would have done better than I.
I tried to take his place in your life.
but I can't "I am sorry son."

I am your mother, I have a place in your life,
but I can't take the place of your father.
I am sorry.
I tried not to look bored at the game for your sake.
But I guess you saw right through me.
You looked at me and asked …
Do you want to leave now?
Is the game boring you?
I felt bad because it was true.

THE ROOT

The root is being uprooted.
The moisture is going dry.
The vine is drying.
The branches are limping.

With teary eyes and a runny nose,
One brave soul spoke the words that are on everyone's mind....
"what are we to do? Who will wipe our tears?"
Who will listen to our groans, moans and complaints.
Who will listen to us?
 Who will share our victories and our failures?

You see, only a mother can understand.
She sees beauty instead of ugliness.
The good instead of the bad.
The brave instead of the coward.
The laughter instead of the sadness.
She criticizes in love and corrects in kindness.

Our names are always on her lips.
With our victories, with our failures and with our,
weakness she takes to God in prayer.
She gives special kinds of hugs, smiles, and kisses.
She cooks better than any other mother.
She is the best!
My mother is special.

Today, knowledge, wisdom and history,
are drifting with her.
Mother, you did not tell me,
who will take care of me.
Who will love me?
Who will take your place?

But can anyone replace a mother?
A mother's love is special.
A mother's love is tender.
It's unconditional.
It's with sacrifice.
It's binding.
It's that love that gives children their wings.
And singers their voices.
Today she is leaving on a journey to be with our Father, God.

She has reports to give about each of us.
I wonder what she will say about me.
"wait Mother, please forgive me"
I told you a lie.
I sold candy.
I meant to give you a call.
I wanted to give you flowers.
I will sing that song you always wanted to hear.
WAIT MOTHER... I love you.

NEVER SHOW YOUR WEAKNESS BEFORE MAN.
SHOW IT TO GOD WHERE YOUR STRENGTH LIES.

NOW IS

I saw you yesterday.
I wanted to tell you that Jesus dies for you and me.
That He loves you and He can forgive you of your sins.
Only if you take time to hear His words.
But you were laughing and talking with friends.
I said, "No you are too busy, it's not the right time.
Today I saw you rushing.
Wait, I must talk to you.
Wait, you have to listen.
But you did not hear me.
I said, there is always tomorrow.
Oh good, tomorrow is Sunday, I will invite you to church
The preacher will preach.
The elders will pray.
The Holy Spirit will move.
And you will be saved.
Then the burden of your salvation will be lifted from my heart.
Then Your Will, will be done Lord.
"No, my child, tomorrow is promised to no one.
Now is the accepted time.
Now is the day of salvation.
Today could be the day his soul is required of him.
Now is the Time.

I SEE

I see doubt creeping in.
By grace, I hold it abay,
I see no need for it.
Faith is what I need.
Depression is knocking at the door.
By grace I did not open the door.
Happiness is what I need.
Temptation is always there.
By Grace I turned aside.
I see no need for it.
Victory is what I need.

WHEN JESUS COMES

When Jesus comes,
He will wipe away all sorrows.
When Jesus comes,
He will take away all pain.
He will give us joy.
He will give us health.
We will clap, sing and shout His praise.
When Jesus comes,
He will receive His own.
When Jesus comes,
He will take us to His glory.
We have come to sup with our King.
Oh! What joy,
What peace divine.
We will sit at His feet.
We will know that we are His and He is ours.
At last, its "Home sweet Home."

ROAD OF LIFE

The Road is Rocky.
I can't walk on it.
Give me wings O Lord, let me fly like an eagle.
The road is long and wide.
I am weak, Lord.
Please give me strength,
Lest I stumble and fall.
The road is weary.
I am tired, Lord.

I need You Lord to hold my hand.
And walk with me through this valley of sin.
Lord, I know it's not only who I am at the end of the road,
But how I made the trip, a sinner or a believer.
Because, you know it all adds up at the end of the road.
How one walks the road really matters in the end.

TAKE MY HAND

I have a valley of my own,
But I will enter yours with you.
You see I have passed through one like yours.
So take my hand, let me walk with you.
I was told to be my brother's keeper.
My valley prepares me to walk with you, to be your keeper.
God has prepared me to do so.
So don't be afraid, my sister or my brother, take my hand.
Let me walk with you.
We are here to bear each other's cross.
Just as Jesus bears the cross for us all.

YOUR WILL

Let Your will be done Lord.
Who am I to say what I want to do or say.
Let Your will, be done Lord.
You are my eyes, ears, feet, and hands.
Please lead me Lord, Your ways are past understanding.

Teach me wisdom to handle situations that confront me,
Day to day.
Give me the peace that passed all understanding.
Let Your will be done Lord. I cannot understand.
But I know Lord, that in the fullness of time,
You, in Your kindness will teach me.

HOLD ON MY CHILD

Hold on my child.
God will carry you through.
He cares for you.
More than you understand.

He understands the pain.
You carry for others.
He wants you to leave them in His hands.

Oh, my child, no one can touch your soul.
It belongs to God.
He protects it day and night.

Praise God my child, He wants you there.
He needs you there at this moment in time.
For what reasons, we do not know.
But one day you will understand.
God's timing is always right.

ABUSE

I stand abused
I stand ashamed.
I stand confused.
I stand alone.
I went to sleep with questions.
Why me?
What did I do to cause this to happen?
The love of my father should not hurt me.
It should not cause me...

PAIN
FEAR
LONELINESS

But why?
Why did he turns on me?
He told me he loved me.
But what he did was not an expression of love.
I stand abused
I stand ashamed
I stand confused.
With questions, but no answer.

WHY

Tiny fingers move across the page.
But the pages are blank.
Words of a hurting heart cannot
Be expressed on paper.
But three letters kept going,
Around and around in the tiny head.
Which belongs to the tiny fingers.
Why?

Tiny lips move, forming the words of pain.
"I was given to you"
"You were supposed to be my loving caretaker."
"I was given to you."
You were supposed to love me.
You were to care for me, not hurt me.
Was I not good enough for you?
Why did you cast me away?

God created me, I am human,
I have feelings.
I scream, why?
As I was ripped from your body.
Do you know the pain of rejection was worse than the burning
of my skin, and the dismembering of my body.
I was given to you.
God, my Father and Creator, made me in His own image.
He chooses you to carry me.
Just as He chooses Mary to carry Jesus, His Son.

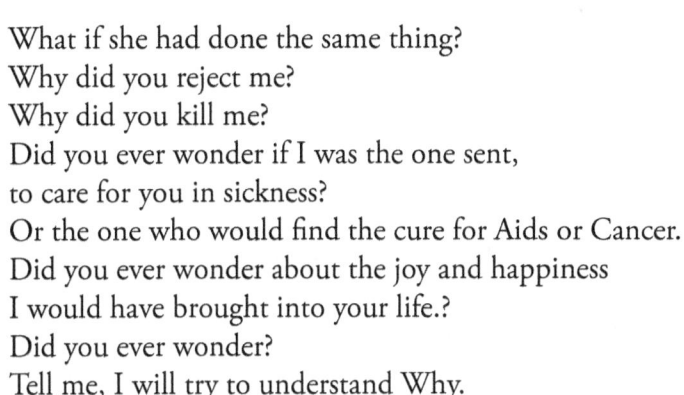

What if she had done the same thing?
Why did you reject me?
Why did you kill me?
Did you ever wonder if I was the one sent,
to care for you in sickness?
Or the one who would find the cure for Aids or Cancer.
Did you ever wonder about the joy and happiness
I would have brought into your life.?
Did you ever wonder?
Tell me, I will try to understand Why.

MY CHILD

My child there is no excuse in this world
Or the next, that can explain my action.
I was alone. Unloved.
Afraid of rejection by my peers.
Afraid, that I would not love and care for you.
I really thought I was doing the best for you.
I was told that there was no you.
So, I did not think that I was killing you.
I am sorry.
Please forgive me.
I look at other children, wondering what you would look like.
I gave you a name.
I would love you and enjoy your company.
Just as I have enjoyed the others I have now.
Please forgive me.
Nights I dream of you, reaching out to me.
But I could never reach you.
I want to hold you and love you.
I want to look in your eyes
I know that your eyes would be the same color as mine.
 Please forgive me, my child.

NEW ORDER FOR A NEW DAY

Clergy from every denomination,
Joined hands with one notion.
To prepare people from every tribe and nation.

They came together with a mission, to create a vision.
Each pledge to aid the elderly.
To educate the men and women of tomorrow,
To give shelter to the homeless,
To set moral standards.
It's a new order for a new day.
They came with arms reaching out to the community.
Regardless of age, sex, religion, race or national origin.

They came with love and compassion
With arms wide open, they formed a circle to fence
In God's people.
A fence made and strengthened by love,
Kindness and compassion.
The fence is the stronghold against the enemies.
The beginning is of God and the end will be of God.
It's a new order for a new day.

WHAT ABOUT ME FATHER

You left me, but you took other children as your own.
You allow them to call you Father.
You hug them.
You kiss them.
But what about me?
You know when they are happy.
And when they are sad.
But what about me?
I am seed of your seed and flesh of your flesh.
I am a reflection of you.
Look at me Dad, I walk, I smile, like you.
I have the same color eyes as yours.

I am a carbon copy of you.
Is that the reason why you don't love me?
Because you don't love yourself?
Give me a chance. I want to love you.
I want to flirt with you as all girls do with their dads.
I want to hear you say to me one day,
"Gosh, my little girl has become a woman."
But you never knew me as a child.
So, it will be hard for you to recognize me as a woman.
Did you ever wonder about me?
Whether I am happy, sad, angry, hungry, sick or lonely.
Did you ever wonder?

Father's day is a sad day.
I imagine you sitting with a little girl on your lap,
Smiling up at you calling you dad.
She is taking my place.
She is taking my dad.
But the worst feeling is knowing that you allow it.

GLORY BE

In all Your glory, we know that You are holy.
You are the great I AM.
You are the Mighty One.
You are the King of Kings.
You are the Lord of Lords.
In all your Glory, you are Holy.

You gave us life that we can worship You.
You are the holy one in all your glory.
Listen to us Dear Lord.
As we humbly worship You.
We love You Dear Lord.
We worship You today.

WHAT IS LOVE

True love knows no color.
True love knows no size.

True love is unexpected.
True love cannot be measured.

True love cannot be contained.
True love is unconditional.

OUR LOVE

Today we share our love with you.
To bask with us in the sunshine of our love.

We declare before God and man that we are in love.
This love was ordained from above.
We hope,
A glimmer of our love will ignite your heart with love.
Our love for each other is unconditional.
So should be yours.

WE WEEP

We weep for you mother, grandmother, mother-in-law, aunt,
cousin, friend we weep.
For lost love,
Carried on the wings of a dove.
For promises unkept.
For expectations unmet,
For this date we rather not have set.
For the love shown to you by some not in life but in death.
We weep,
Yes, we weep while you sleep.
For all the hurt you have been through.
For all the pain we may have caused you.
We weep,
Yes, we weep for your forgiveness.
We weep as the tears cleanse your heart of its sorrows.
We weep.
As we shared your love, joy, humbleness and gratitude.
We weep for the many values from which to borrow.
As we seek a better tomorrow
Yes, we weep to cleanse the heart and the soul.
For the tears to water the garden of your heart.
For us to reap the Fruits of the Spirit to embed in our hearts that
we weep no more.

LOVE

LOVE, you come within my reach.
But I cannot hold you.
LOVE, you have touched the tips of my fingers,
But never the center of my hands.
I cannot hold you.
LOVE, why do you keep giving me a sip,
But never a drink.?
Why the bittersweet? Why not the honey?
LOVE, "oh what? have I enslaved you in my heart?"
Well, I guess you needed to be free.
With wings of a soaring eagle.
With the trust of a newborn.
Like a sunrise in all its glory.
Like the beauty of a rose that rises above the thorns.
Like a blue cloudless sky giving peace.
Like that special glance between a man and a woman,
That warms and quivers the heart.
Like that tender touch and soft word that melts anger.
LOVE, YES. There should be no demand or bondage on me.Set
me free like the perpetual circles that ripple forth in water,
Pierced by a stone.
It's in giving that you will receive, and I am more effective when
I am shared with my three companions:
Trust, Respect, and Forgiveness.

MILLION DOLLAR

I finally asked the million-dollar question.
Who is my Father?
Where is my Father?
I waited with great expectation for the answers.
To my questions.
The silence was long.
Did the phone line die?
No, there was breathing at the other end.
Then a voice filled with pain and fear said,
"I was raped"
I don't know your father."
"what! I am the result of rape?"
Tears filled my eyes.
My heart was heavy with pain.
I am nobody.
I was not born into a loving family.
I was not wanted by anyone.
I am the result of rape.
Conceived in fear and trembling.
No love, no joy, only terror
Who am I really?
I am so in complete.
 Only one parent, filled with anger and resentment,
 Filled with shame.
I am a person with an incomplete name.
An incomplete root, no sense of belonging.
As tears came running down,
I looked up to Jesus, He spoke
"You are complete in Me, take Me as your
Father and Mother."

TIME HURRIES BY

Time hurries by
As you stand still, waiting for tomorrow.
Longing for yesterday.
But today is yours.
Now is the time
To laugh
To cry.
To reach out to someone.
To say I love you
To forgive and receive love.
To understand and offer peace.
Now is the time.
Don't wait, today will soon be yesterday.
And tomorrow is promised to no one.

Now is the time to share a cheerful word.
Share thoughts of wisdom and understanding.
To share joy and peace that comes from a special relationship
with Jesus.
But most of all, now is the time to share God's word
 With someone, anyone, everyone
Don't be selfish; share, tell, give.
There is more than enough in God's Kingdom
To go around.
Do what you can today.
Because there might be no
Tomorrow.

A CANOPY OF LOVE

SHE CAME
As a gift of love from our FATHER above.
She came as a tower of strength for all.

SHE CAME
With the gift of motherhood full of wisdom to understand each
child in their own unique way.
Her heart was more than enough to hold each one dear.

SHE LIVED
With a canopy of love, she enfolds her husband, family and
friends.
She remained steadfast in her faith without wavering.
In the midst of pain, she pours into others.
Her gentleness when needed.
Her kindness always
Her intensity when necessary.
She was a tower of strength to all, using the love of Christ.
She went through the fire and came out as pure gold.

SHE LEFT
She heard her new name, and she answered. She went home,
as gift to her Savior.
She sang a new song of praise to Him.
Her time of everlasting life, without sorrow or pain had begun.

SHE SPOKE
Cry not for me. Rejoice with me.
Pour love and forgiveness into each other.
Embrace the Lord. That where I am you will be also.
I spoke, Good bye my friend.

AND THEY CRIED

And they cried,
O' Lord where are You?
"Hear my cry, hold my hand.
The pain is too much, the knowing is too great."

And they cried.
Where is my mother to hold, to cry with me?
Where is my father to protect me; to care for me?
Where is love? Did it take flight?
Where is justice? None for me?

Each shed tears to wash away the hurt.
Hurt that stick like tar to the open wound.
Each cried, why!? With soundless voice of hurt.
Each moan, too numb to form words.
Each cried 'why?'
Wordlessness along with the tears, the pain, the hurt.
Each has a unique story, yet common to all.

Why father?
You were supposed to love me, to care for me.
 not hurting me, not abuse me.
But to protect me from what you have done to me.
God entrusted you with my life.
I trusted you with my love.
You destroyed both.
And you call yourself a man? a father?

Mother! How could you?
You saw the wrong, yet you did not stop it.
You did not help me.
You slept with him all knowing, not caring; not saying.
And now you cry "Why?"
What emotion propels your tears …hate or disappointment?

And she cried,

I went with him as he took my hand, speaking words of care.
While thinking things he should not dare.
I am a child; how could I know that he would have hurt me so.
Why? I did not know you; you did not know me.
I did no wrong.
Why did you choose to rape and kill me?
I am just a little girl, a boy.
Wanting only to be loved
Wanting only to play with my brother, sister, and friend.

And he cried,

I begged him to let me go.
Not to hurt me so.
He did not speak; he did not resemble the person who had just
laughed with me, ate with me.
 He was filled with thoughts of kill.
He was a stranger to me as he raised the knife to take my last
breath.
I cried, "O Lord, please help me I am here just a little while.
Just learning to love, to trust, to care."

I cried.

I felt the blade of the knife as it pierced my heart.
Taking my last breath.
The one I wanted to use to ask why?
Yet in the stillness of my being; I know there is no reason for a
father to kill,
Especially his own.

You kill as a stranger unknown to me.
I died knowing that my father near and dear to me had taken
the light from my life.
Now darkness hovers, with no tears to wash away the anguish.
As the question why? lingers in the stillness of my being.

Evil has moved man to wage war on the helpless, the weak,
Each has lost hope and dreams.
Death has become their reality.
'Why' was not important anymore.
The voices are still.

MIRACLES

The God of Miracles reaches out His hand. I took it.
Instantly, scars fell from my eyes, and I beheld my Savior.
The splendor of heaven was a sight to behold.
Earthly words cannot describe.
Now I understand why my miracle happened here and not
there.
I needed my sight for here, not there.
Every pain, sorrow, and happiness
I experienced on earth is now enfold in one word GLORY!

My tears turned to joy the moment the Hand of Miracles
Touched mine.
I am with whom my soul loves.
Cry you must but have no regrets.
Instead, love, forgive, share, help, embrace and care for each
other.
Give more of you to the Lord, it is worth it.
Cry not for me, my time on earth are now memories,
Hold them dear.
I am awaiting my new name.
I am now a citizen of the Holy Nation.

HE KNOWS

I cried.
He read my tears.
He read the confusion of emotions in my tears.

With blessed hope, He wipes away my tears.
With His passion of pure love, His goodness overwhelms me,
His mercy which is ever present kept me in His grace.
Allowing His favors to surround me.

I sang praises to the Lord.
He knew my joy in praising Him.
So, His presence was filled with my gift of worship.

MY LORD

As He read tears
He was full of compassion.
My tears, He wipes away with His blessed hope.
His pure love overwhelms me.

His goodness follows me wherever I go.
His every flowing mercy kept me.
His benefits towards me are renewed each day.
His favors surround me.

He shed his blood to protects me.
He wipes away my tears, reminding me of His promise.
"Low I am with you always"
And all He asked of me, is to Praise Him.

A LOAN FROM GOD

This is mine.
This is yours.
Yet, nothing belongs to us.
Everything is a loan from God.
The Creator of all.

There are those that boast of their worldly goods.
Not willing to share.
Not willing to hear that all good things come from heaven above.
Not understanding that none belongs to them,
It's all a loan from God.

THE GREAT 'I AM'

My Lord, You are,
My hope
My trust
My help
My rock
My love
My fortress
My protector
My creator
My healer
My friend
My father
My brother
My master
My mother
My refuge
My savior
My strong tower
My only redeemer
My strong habitation
Jesus, My Lord is the Great "I AM" of my life.

HE WAS GIVEN THE TIME

He was given the time.
To seek forgiveness.
To know the great' I AM'
To find peace with God and man.

He was given the time.
To walk with Jesus.
To celebrate a new life.
To find new faith in Christ.

He was given the time
To choose the path that he should take.
To tell of his newfound joy.

He was given the time
To share fun memories of the past.
To embrace the joys of his grands and great-grands.
To tell of his love for each kinfolk.

He was given the time.
He took it.
Nearing the end of his time,
He said, "I am a winner"
He knew that at the end of this time,
Is the beginning of time eternal.
He came into the knowledge that,
To be absent from the body
Is to be present with the Lord.
He knew that the time that has no end, has begun.

A MOMENT IN TIME.

No words were spoken.
We might not have understood each other.
Yet we smiled.
Our spirits spoke to each other.
And a moment in time began.
For a moment two hearts become one.

A moment, that took us on a journey of emotions.
A moment that marks the beginning of our lives together.
A moment we now wish to celebrate with you.
This moment is special,
It covers our faults.
It gives life to our laughter.
It protects, gives and receives.
This moment is ordained from heaven above, covered by God's
blessings.
Today we honor your presence by our pledge to you.
That the greatest moment of love will always be there in our
lives.
A kiss, a smile, a kind look, a sincere compliment.
This moment of love is the best gift of all.

MY JESUS LOVE

I walk towards Jesus
He opens His arms to receive me.
He said, "you have been loved before you were conceived,
I love you my daughter, for you I died."

I took His hand.
And my life changed.
"Behold I make all things new," said Jesus.
A new love gave birth within my heart.
I found love in every problem.
In everyone, in every sorrow.

The joy of His love sustains me.
The peace in His love maintains me.
His love taught me how to love.
The love of Jesus never fails.

TEARS

Tears have no language for human.
Yet it speaks.
It has no feeling.
It shows happiness
It expresses grief.

It knows when the heart is broken.
It knows when love overflows the heart.
It knows when to cleanse the heart.

A tear can be wiped away.
With a smile
With good thoughts
With a kind word
With a hug
With a kiss.
Tears have a language of their own.

To Receive Jesus as your Savior

Dear Heavenly Father,

I come to you in the name of Jesus, Your word says, "'... him that cometh to me I will in no way Cast out" (John 6:37).

Lord, I recognize that I am a sinner. I Ask you to forgive me of my sins, according to your word." Your word also says, "... if thou shalt confess with thy mouth the Lord Jesus, and shalt believe in thine heart that God hath raised him from the dead, thou shalt be saved." "For whosoever shall call upon the name of the Lord shall be saved:" (Romans 10:9-13). I believe in my heart that Jesus Christ is the son of God. I believe he was raised from the dead for justification; I am calling on the name of Jesus to receive the gift of salvation.

If you say this prayer and in faith believe, you are now a child of God. We praise God with you.

The Whys Of The Poems

Behind each of these poems there is a story.

The Cry is dedicated to everyone with AIDS, especially to those that have not accepted Jesus as their Savior.

Grace giving God praise that one day by grace, we who accepted Him will be in glory.

God is able, take heart, he cares when there is trouble, these poems reassure us that regardless of what, God is greater than any problem.

Your will God's will must be the desire of every Christian. This poem is appealing to God to teach, lead and show us His will.

True love, our love, what is love is dedicated to All who have truly loved.

Hold on my child, I dedicate this poem to all the Teachers, pastors, missionaries and all the workers, of God's kingdom.

What about me father, this poem is dedicated to all Those young ladies who long to be a part of their father's life.

Alone, this was a period in my life when I was very depressed. I started to write how I felt at that moment, God finished it by writing His own words.

Take my hands, our life experiences prepare us to, help others. We should always strive to be our brother's Keeper.

I am yours, giving yourself to God gives you all the right to the kingdom of God.

No ordinary citizen A reminder to every Christian of Our purpose, our mission and where we belong.

In my time is dedicated to a little boy I met at Benny Hinn's Church service. He wanted so much to be healed.

Now is, so many times the Holy Spirit gives us the, Opportunity to tell someone of God's love, but we fail to do so.

Father 's day is dedicated to all who do not know their earthly father or mother.

NOTE: I met my father in 2021 at the age of 68years.

I see to live a victorious life in Christ, one must be aware that doubt, and depression has no place in our lives. Defeating temptation is a step towards victory.

When Jesus comes what better hope can we have than the coming of our Lord and Savior.

Mend my heart, at times one's heart feels like it has just Gone through the shredder, and we must remember that Only God can mend a broken heart.

Love 'love', wonderful love, how can something so beautiful Hurt so much?' We must give thanks to God for His unconditional love.

A piece of clay, take a piece of clay in your hand, look at it and look at yourself in the mirror. That should remind you of How great and awesome our CREATOR GOD is.

Soulmate, so many people need and seek love and companionship, but do not seem to know how to attain it.

The root, children cried at funerals for different reasons but those who never give or care seem to cry the most. It is so sad when we fail to appreciate our parents.

The empty chair is dedicated to my sons, Leron and Alrick and to all the boys who grew up in a single mother's home.

Messenger of love is dedicated to Mother Theresa and to everyone who serves the greater good.

Why is dedicated to all the children who are aborted.

Million dollar is dedicated to all who are born because of rape.

My child is for all the women who are truly sorry about aborting their children

He was given the time, this poem is dedicated to my friend's father who accepted Jesus at age eighty -two about six months before he passed away.

Miracles, we weep, a conopy of love are dedicated to my loved ones who I truly miss.

Author Biography

Pauline J. Schloss-Esbery A poet and author has written and published books on various topics. She has published four books of poems, and a book on the principles of tithing:
'Tithing –The Holy Seed'

The aim of this book, "The Voices of the Heart", is to bring to light hidden life issues of the heart. To encourage others to accept and celebrate Christ, to keep happy memories of loved ones who are departed.

Originally from Jamaica, Ms. Schloss-Esbery has made South Florida her home for many years. She attended Church Teacher's College: Mandeville in Jamaica, she taught there for many years. At age forty-seven she attended Trinty International University and later St. Thomas University in Miami where she graduated Cum Laude In the field of psychology. She gained some life experiences from her trips to thirty-four countries on five of the seven continents.

She is the mother of six children and a grandmother of seven granddaughters and seven grandsons. She also wears the hat of mother-in-law and stepmother with much love.

Her passions are writing, traveling, cooking and fulfilling the 'Great Commission'.

"I am driven by a deep passion and need to make a difference and leave this world a little better than when I arrived. That's what keeps me going"

Rick HansenCC. O.B.C.